LIVES
AND
TIMES

Pocahontas

Margaret Hudson

Heinemann
LIBRARY

First published in Great Britain by Heinemann Library
Halley Court, Jordan Hill, Oxford OX2 8EJ,
a division of Reed Educational and Professional Publishing Ltd.
Heinemann is a registered trademark of Reed Educational & Professional Publishing Limited.

OXFORD FLORENCE PRAGUE MADRID ATHENS
MELBOURNE AUCKLAND KUALA LUMPUR SINGAPORE TOKYO
IBADAN NAIROBI KAMPALA JOHANNESBURG GABORONE
PORTSMOUTH NH (USA) CHICAGO MEXICO CITY SAO PAULO

Designed by Ken Vail Graphic Design, Cambridge
Illustrations by Shirley Tourett
Printed in Hong Kong / China

02 01 00 99 98
10 9 8 7 6 5 4 3 2 1

ISBN 0 431 02488 X

Some words are shown in bold, **like this**. You can find out what they mean by looking in the glossary. The glossary also helps you say difficult words.

British Library Cataloguing in Publication Data

Hudson, Margaret
Pocahontas. - (Lives & times)
1. Pocahontas, ca. 1595–1617 - Juvenile literature 2. Indian women - North American - Biography - Juvenile literature 3. Indians of North America - Virginia - Biography - Juvenile literature
I. Title
975 .5'01'092

Acknowledgements

The Publishers would like to thank the following for permission to reproduce photographs:

Ashmolean Museum p17; Borough Council of King's Lynn and West Norfolk, courtesy of Mrs Alex Stevenson p21; British Library p22; British Museum pp18, 19; The Kobal Collection p23; National Portrait Gallery, Smithsonian Institute p20.

Cover photograph reproduced with permission of National Portrait Gallery.

Our thanks to Betty Root for her comments in the preparation of this book.

Every effort has been made to contact copyright holders of any material reproduced in this book. Any omissions will be rectified in subsequent printings if notice is given to the Publisher.

Contents

The first part of this book tells you the story of Pocahontas.
The second part tells you how we can find out about her life.

Early life

Pocahontas was born in America, in about 1596. Her father was an **Indian** king. He was called Powhatan.

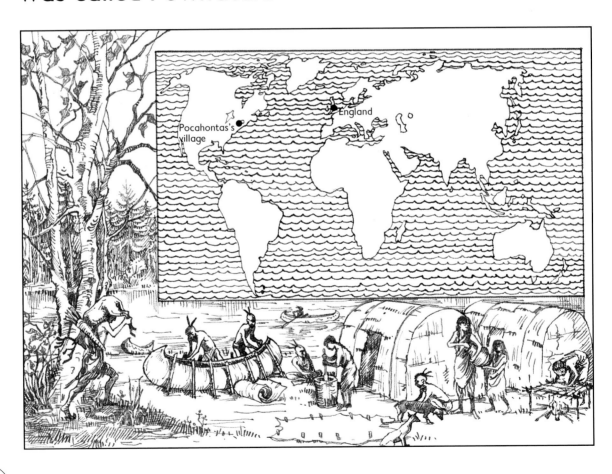

When Pocahontas was 10 years old, some
English people came to live in America.
They built a town called Jamestown near
her village.

The English

Pocahontas visited the town. She taught the English her **language** and they taught her English.

The English gave the **Indians** tools and pots. In return, the Indians gave the English food.

Helping the sick

The **Indians** and the English did not always trust each other. They argued over food and land. Sometimes they fought.

That winter, the English ran out of food and became ill. Pocahontas asked her father to send them food, which he did.

Saving a life

Soon the **Indians** and the English were
fighting again. An Englishman, called
John Smith, was caught by the Indians.
They wanted to kill him.

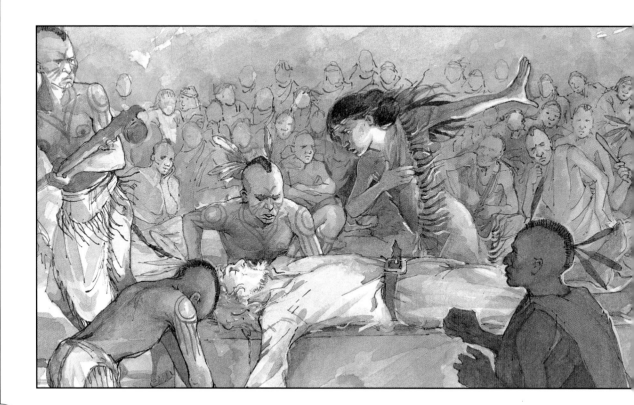

John Smith had made friends with
Pocahontas when she visited Jamestown.
She stopped the Indians from killing him
and they let him go.

Marriage

Pocahontas went to live with the English when she was about 17. She hoped it would stop them fighting each other.

About a year later, in 1614, Pocahontas married an Englishman called John Rolfe. She was 19 when she gave birth to their son, Thomas. At last her father, Powhatan, stopped fighting the English.

England

Pocahontas was now called Rebecca Rolfe. In 1616, she left America and sailed to England with her husband and son. She met King James I and many other important people.

When it was time to go home, Pocahontas became ill. She died at Gravesend before the ship sailed. She was only 21 years old.

Artefacts

There are many different things from the time that tell us about Pocahontas and her life.

This **cloak** was made by the **Indians**. It was sent from Powhatan to King James I of England as a present.

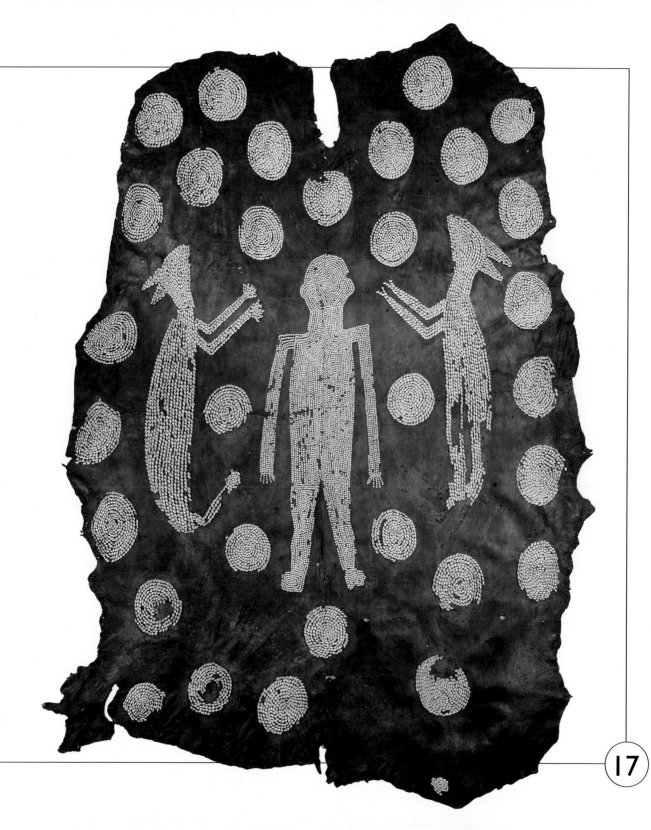

17

Pictures

An Englishman called John White drew these pictures in 1584. They show life in **Indian** villages like the one Pocahontas lived in.

The towne of Pomeiock and true forme of their howses, couered and enclosed some wth matts, and some wth barcks of trees. All compassed abowt wth smale poles stock thick together in stedd of a wall.

The Indians used branches to make the shapes of their houses. Then they covered them with mats made from **reeds**.

Portraits

We know what Pocahontas looked like. These pictures of her were painted when she visited England in 1616.

Ætatis suæ 21. A°. 1616.

The boy in this picture is her son, Thomas Rolfe. He was about two years old when this **portrait** was painted.

Books and films

We know what Pocahontas did because people wrote about it at the time. This book was written by John Smith, the man Pocahontas saved.

The story of Pocahontas is still told today.

Glossary

This glossary explains difficult words, and helps you to say words which are hard to say.

artefacts things which survive from the past that tell us more about it

cloak a coat with no sleeves that you wrap around yourself

Indians people who lived in America before white people went to live there

language the words people in one country use to speak to each other

Pocahontas You say *poe-ka-hon-tas*

portrait picture of a real person

Powhatan You say *pow-ha-tan*

reeds special long grasses which grow near water

Index

24